EDEXCEL GCSE POETRY ANTHOLOGY
COLLECTION D: BELONGING

CONTENTS

CONTENTS 1
About the Author 2
About this Guide 3
THE POEMS 16
To My Sister – William Wordsworth 18
Sunday Dip – John Clare 24
Mild the mist upon the hill – Emily Bronte 28
Captain Cook (To My Brother) – Letitia Elizabeth Landon 32
Clear and Gentle Stream – Robert Bridges 39
I Remember, I Remember 43
Island Man– Grace Nichols 47
Peckham Rye Lane – Amy (A.K.) Blakemore 51
We Refugees – Benjamin Zephaniah 56
US – Zaffar Kunial 61
In Wales, wanting to be Italian – Imtiaz Dhakher 65
Kumukanda – Kayo Chingonyi 68
Jamaican British – Raymond Antrobus 72
My Mother's Kitchen – Choman Hardi 77
The Emigrée – Carol Rumens 81
Links, Connections, Comparisons & the Unseen Poem 86
Rhythm in English Verse 95

About the Author

After graduating from Oxford University with a degree in English Language and Literature, and 26 years working for British Airways, I decided to train as a teacher of English. For the next ten years, I taught in the secondary state sector in a multi-cultural and socio-economically diverse area west of London. On my retirement in 2016, I was second in the English department, co-ordinator of the A Level English Literature curriculum and Lead Year 13 tutor, co-ordinating university entrance applications. I am also an Examiner for AQA GCSE English Literature.

My approach to studying poetry is straightforward: unless you understand *what is happening* in the poem – the event, incident or story – about which the poet weaves his literary magic, there can be no understanding of a poet's literary techniques. The two are inextricably intertwined. There is a LOT of very variable analyses of poetry on the internet. Much of it stems from a failure to understand *what is happening*. This failure leads to students having a rattle-bag of literary terminology but with nothing on which to hang it. Naming metric forms and rhyme schemes, and poetic techniques, with no understanding of why the poet has used them, is a waste of time. It also leads to spurious, and erroneous, analyses of structure and form. I have read, in exam papers, that the *"shape of the line on the page, if you turn it sideways, corresponds to the furrows of a field."* Or, *"the varied line length suggests the outline of the Manhattan skyline"*. Students do not come up with ideas like this unless there is a fundamental failure to grasp the links between *substance* (the *"what is happening"*) and *structure* (rhythm and rhyme) and *language* (the words used).

This guide is an attempt to make these links and help students appreciate why a poem has been written in the way that it has

About this Guide

The Guide has been written primarily for students of GCSE English Literature as specified by EDEXCEL in the post-2015 syllabus (1ET0). It addresses the requirement to study one cluster of poems taken from the *EDEXCEL/Pearson Poetry Anthology* and the requirement to analyse and compare two Unseen poems. These requirements are assessed in Component 2 (19th century Novel and Poetry since 1789), Section B: Poetry, and Section C: Unseen Poetry, of the examination.

The Guide aims to address Assessment Objectives AO1, AO2 and AO3 for the examination of this component, namely:

AO1: Read, understand and respond to texts. Students should be able to:
- maintain a critical style and develop an informed personal response
- use textual references, including quotations, to support and illustrate interpretations. *[1]

---

[1] *Whilst there is no specific mention of "*making comparisons*", the mark scheme makes it clear that the examiners expect the essay response to be "*comparative*", described as "*Critical, exploratory comparison*" at the highest band.

AO2: Analyse the language, form and structure used by a writer to create meanings and effects, using relevant subject terminology where appropriate.

AO3: Show understanding of the relationships between texts and the contexts in which they were written.

The poems are explored individually, with links and connections between them drawn as appropriate. The format of each exploration is similar:

- An explanation of key features of the poem that require contextual knowledge or illustration and the relationship between the text and its context.
- A summary of the key themes of the poems, with a note on possible thematic links to other poems in the cluster
- A brief summary of the metric form, rhyme scheme or other structural features, related to the theme
- A "walk-through" (or explication) of the poem, ensuring that what is happening in the poem is understood, how the rhythm and rhyme contribute to meaning, an explanation of the meaning of words which may be unfamiliar, an exploration of language and imagery and a comment on main themes.

A note on "themes" (AO1 task)

The question (or *task*) in the examination for *Component 2 (19th century Novel and Poetry since 1789), Section B: Poetry,* will be on a theme which may form the focus of the poem or be an integral part of its meaning. You will be asked to make a comparative exploration of the presentation of this *"theme"* in one named poem and one other poem of your choice from the collection.

Section C: Unseen Poetry will ask you to explore the presentation of a given *"theme"* in an Unseen poem and compare it to the treatment of the same *theme* in a second Unseen poem.

Given that Collection D: is titled *"Belonging"*, you can expect to be asked to explore various ideas and perspectives on this theme. This could include, but not be limited to, the various kinds of *belonging* presented in the Collection, as in belonging to a family, a country, a culture, or a group of people who share common experiences and/or values. It could ask for an exploration of a relevant **emotion** – such as anger, loss, sorrow, nostalgia, confusion; the **evocation of "place"**, as the subject of the poem, or as the setting for the poem; the treatment of **abstract concepts** such as Time, Loyalty, Absence, Conflict, Culture or Religion; a "**happening**" such as Birth, Childhood, Emigration, Separation; types of **relationships between people, or between people and places,** such as unsatisfactory, jealous, obsessive, changing, confusing. The range is very broad.

Where a poem from the anthology lends itself to suggesting a particular theme, this has been noted in the overview and linked to other poems which have similar themes. However, these suggestions are illustrative, not exhaustive; one of the skills to be mastered is to know the texts well enough to be able to link them to themes which may not be immediately obvious. Students should spend some time mapping the links between poems thematically and illustrating how these themes are treated in similar or differing ways.

As well as links of *theme,* links and connections should be made between *narrative voice, form, structure* and *language.* At the end of this book are some questions which should be considered when making links and connections, and when analysing the Unseen poem(see *"Links and Connections."*)

A note on "relevant subject terminology" (AO1)

This means the *semantic field* of literary criticism, or "jargon". Criticism has a language to describe the features peculiar to the study of literature, just as football has words to describe manoeuvres and equipment – *"penalty"*, *"off-side"*, *"wing"*, *"long cross"*, *"throw-in"*. To be able to critique literature, you need to know this language and use it correctly. Throughout this guide, literary terminology has been *italicised*, indicating that these words need to become part of your vocabulary when discussing the texts and writing essays. For illustration, here are some very basic literary terms that are often carelessly used and will make your writing in exams less effective if you do not apply them correctly.

Text – is the printed words. The *whole text* is all the words that are identified, usually by a *title*, as belonging together as an integral piece of writing.

A *book* is a collection of printed pages bound together to make a *whole text*. A *book* can be any text – fiction, non-fiction; play, novel; car maintenance manual, encyclopaedia. A *book* is a **physical** entity, like "*DVD*" or "*scroll*", not a creative one.

A *novel* is a particular kind of text – a *genre*. It is characterised by certain creative features, such as being *fictional,* usually *narrative in structure* and with various *characters* who do things, or have things happen to them. It may be *descriptive* and may contain *dialogue*.

A *novella* is a short novel. Its scope and the number of characters are often (but not always) more limited than in a novel.

A *short story* is a narrative fiction, of variable, but limited length.

A play is another *genre*. It is designed to be performed and watched, rather than read. It can be *fictional* or *non-fictional*, or a mixture. It is predominantly made up of *dialogue* between *characters*, although there may be descriptive elements within this *dialogue* and in the *stage directions*.

A *poem* is a particular *genre* which is characterised by the deliberate, and recurring, use of *rhythm* and *rhyme* and/or by a particular attention to *diction*, in the form of *word-choice* and *imagery*. It is opposed to *prose*. However, there are *poetical* prose writers whose language uses the distinctive features of poetry – such as *alliteration*, *rhythm* and *imagery*.

Beyond these simple definitions, there are a host of other literary terms. These terms have been used where they are necessary to describe features of the texts and are defined on the first usage, and subsequently when repeated, depending on how common the usage and the relevance to the poem under discussion.

There is a trend towards teaching students grammatical terms – such as the parts of speech – and using these in essays, in the mistaken belief that these will gain marks under use of *"subject terminology"*. This achieves very little. The feedback from the Examining Boards make it clear that linguistic analyses, including analysis of parts of speech, have little merit when demonstrating *critical understanding*. It is also better to avoid using subject terminology if you are unsure of its exact meaning.

A note on "critical comparisons" (AO1)

The new specification refers to *"links and connections"* as well as *"comparisons"* between literary texts. There is little to be gained from making, often spurious, comparisons which fail to illuminate the text, and structuring essays which say *"on the one hand/ on the other"*. The highest band marks challenge the student to be able to *synthesise* their knowledge of the texts – a higher level skill. The Mark Scheme refers to: *"critical, exploratory, well-structured comparison"*. Further guidance on this is given in the section on *"Links and Connections"*.

A note on "create meanings and effects" (AO2)

There are very few marks to be gained by simply spotting and correctly naming literary techniques. Even fewer if those terms are used incorrectly. It is better NOT to use a literary term at all than use the wrong one. **NEVER build an essay around literary techniques; you need to focus your essay on the thematic question (the "*task*"), showing how form, language and structure contribute to meaning**. Comments on literary techniques **must** be linked to purpose and meaning to gain marks in the higher bands. This principle has been followed in the analyses of the texts. Not all literary techniques used by the poets are discussed in the commentaries; only those that are particularly relevant to the discussion of meaning, form or theme have been explored.

You are also required to know something about *metric form* – the use of rhythm and the terms which are used to describe it – and relate the use of *metre* to meaning. Metre has been explained in the commentaries. Stressed beats are in **bold** and the *metric feet* are shown with the / symbol. "*A Note on Metre*" has been given at the end of this guide, which explains the main metric forms used, with examples from the texts.

Finally, you need to know when form and structure are used *for effect* and when the choice of a form or structure is part of a poetic tradition or a feature of a poetic movement (e.g. *Romantic, Modern*). Sometimes poets write in *sonnet* form because they like writing sonnets; they are following a tradition; it was expected by their readers at the time of writing. Similarly, with choices of metre. Both *iambic pentametre* and *ballad form* (alternating lines of *iambic tetrametre* and *iambic trimetre*) are common metric forms used by very many poets of different eras because it was a common form for poetry. It *may* be valid to link the choice of metric form to the poet's theme and it *may* be that the poet uses the metric form within the poem for effect. However, making far-fetched and spurious connections between choice of form and theme are largely a waste of time. Sometimes a *sonnet* is just a *sonnet*. However, *how* (rather than *why*) the sonnet form is used in a poem should be explored. For example, where the *volta* occurs, the use of rhyme and the use of *rhyming couplets*, and these choices related to meaning.

A note on "relationship between texts and context" (AO3)

There is a requirement to have some knowledge of the biographical, social-economic, political or literary context in which these poems were written **and show how this is reflected in the text.** "Context" is also taken to mean *"ideas and perspectives"*. This may include understanding the relationship between the specific themes of the poem and the more general attitudes of society at the time. Edexcel has given further guidance:

- *the author's own life and individual situation, including the place and time of writing, only where these relate to the text*
- *the historical setting, time and location of the text*
- *social and cultural contexts (e.g., attitudes in society; expectations of different cultural groups)*
- *the literary context of the text, for example, literary movements or genres*
- *the way in which texts are received and engaged with by different audiences, at different times (for example, how a text may be read differently in the twenty-first century from when it was written).*

Understanding of meaning is enriched by knowing relevant autobiographical details, particularly where the subject matter focuses on relationships. Many poems use allusions and references to classical mythology, the Bible, popular culture and general knowledge, without which meaning is obscure and appreciation limited.

Relevant contextual information has been given for each poem in either the introduction under "**Context**" or in the analyses.

A note on *typography*

Typography is the way the words of the poems are printed on the page. Remember – most poems, until relatively recently, were written by hand and therefore the look of a poem on the page when it is printed is not necessarily an indication of intent by the poet – it may be the *typography*. There are conventions in *typography* for poems which are adhered to by certain editions but ignored in others. For example, many of the pre-1900 poems start each line with a capital letter. This is of no significance – it is a typographical choice. Similarly, whether lines are indented or blocked may be typographical, rather than meaningful. Similarly, line length is often a feature of *metre*. Check that a line is, in fact, "longer" metrically before commenting on it. You should always look for other, supporting, evidence if you are going to make any link between layout on the page and meaning.

Capitalisation of individual words in a poem may be deliberate. Pre-1900 poets often capitalised virtues, as in Truth, Beauty, Purity or Nature. You should be able to tell whether capitalisation is a printing convention, or for a purpose, from the context. Where this is critical to understanding, it has been mentioned in the commentaries.

You will see in the older poems that the final *"-ed"* of the past tense of verbs may be depicted as *"'d"*, as in *"Volley'd and thunder'd"* in *"The Charge of the Light Brigade"*. This is simply to indicate that the words should be pronounced as two syllables. Sometimes, to make a full metric line, they would have been pronounced as three: *"thun-de-red"*. Alternatively, words which are usually pronounced as a single syllable were sometimes elongated to two, to complete a metric line. This was indicated by an accent symbol above the second syllable. However, this does not appear to have been standardised in the Collection. So, in "*A Poison Tree*", line 7 should have an accent on "*sunned*", as it would have been pronounced "*sun-néd*" to complete the metric line: ***And** I/**sun**-néd/**it** with/smiles.*

Preparing for the Unseen Poems

The best preparation for this component of the examination is to read, and listen to, poetry of all kinds, regularly. There are websites which will deliver a "*poem-a-day*" to your mobile. These two combine contemporary American poetry with classics:
https://www.poets.org/poetsorg/poem-day
https://www.poetryfoundation.org/newsletter
The Poetry Foundation website enables you to browse poems clustered by theme. This is a particularly useful feature to enable you to practise comparing poems.

How to use this Guide

As the modern poems within the anthology are copyrighted to the authors, it has not been possible to print them within this Guide. You will therefore need to read the commentaries with a copy of the text alongside. However, the poems have been quoted in places for illustrative purposes. Where the poems are out of copyright, they have been quoted at greater length.

Bibliography

Edexcel have published supporting materials for the Collection which are available to teachers.

Further reading on context can be found on the following useful websites:

http://www.bl.uk/romantics-and-victorians/articles/the-romantics#

The British Library has a number of articles in their Discovery section on modern literature.

www.victorianweb.org

Many of the modern poets have their own websites, which are worth exploring for autobiographical details and commentaries on their poems.

THE POEMS

To My Sister – William Wordsworth

Context

Wordsworth (1770-1855) was a year older than his sister, Dorothy, to whom he was very close throughout his adult life. On the death of their mother, as children they were intermittently separated, but lived together from 1795 until William's death. Dorothy was a diarist and writer but largely unpublished in her lifetime. Her *"Grasmere Journal"*, an account of day-to-day life in the Lake District, was published in 1897.

The poem was written in 1798 whilst they were living in the Quantock Hills in Somerset, the first place designated as an Area of Outstanding Natural Beauty. Living with them was Basil Montague, the infant son of a widowed friend, who appears as *"Edward"* in the poem. Living nearby was Samuel Taylor Coleridge, with whom Wordsworth compiled the first volume of the *"Lyrical Ballads"* (1798) which is seen as the defining work of the early Romantic Movement.

Like other Romantic poets (Blake, Byron, Coleridge, Keats and Shelley), William Wordsworth challenges the supremacy of rational, scientific thought, seeking for spirituality and the transforming power of the imagination in human lives. The Romantics took themselves seriously as men who, through their poetry, could help others understand the world around them. The creative process and the workings of the imagination were worth exploration in themselves, giving us an insight into our relationship to our place in the physical world around us (loosely defined as "Nature") and how we might tap into powers beyond the merely physical. In another age, this could be equated with "religion", but the Romantics were, primarily, atheists and did not equate this awareness of spirituality with any established religion.

Themes

These ideas are present in this poem. Although Wordsworth dedicates the poem to Dorothy, the focus is as much on his desire to share with her the transformative power of the Natural World as it is to present a pen portrait of her and their relationship:

*"And from the blessed power that rolls
About, below, above,
We'll frame the measure of our souls:
They shall be tuned to love".*

The "**Belonging**" here is not just to one another, as siblings, but to a larger whole - the natural world (*"blessed power"*) to which they are "tuned in" as it embraces them. This idea recurs in Bronte's *"Mild the mist"*, where she shows a similar sense of belonging to the landscape around her and also in Island Man, where the sounds of nature come to him in his dreams.

Form, language and structure

Although not included in the *"Lyrical Ballads"*, this poem shares characteristics with them. Wordsworth set out to reclaim English poetry from the *"gaudiness and inane phraseology of modern writers"*[2] and explore whether: *"the language of conversation in the middle and lower classes of society is adapted to the purposes of poetic pleasure"*. The ballads are characterised by the use of the *ballad form,* simple language, and everyday subject matter. However, they are far from simple in either their form or their ideas. They are highly crafted, using various verse forms, and use the everyday events to consider philosophical ideas about Man's position in the universe.

Ballad form is a variant of *common metre* , which strictly has alternate lines of four stressed beats (*tetrametres*) and three stressed beats (*trimetres*)[3]. *Ballad form* tends to be less rigid, as in this poem. In stanza 1, and throughout, the first three lines have four stressed beats (*tetrametres*) and the last has three (*trimetres*). The stressed beats are in **bold**:

*It **is** the **first** mild **day** of **March**:*
*Each **min**ute **sweet**er **than** be**fore***
*The **red**breast **sings** from the **tall larch***
*That **stands** be**side** our **door**.*

Notice also that the pattern of unstressed and stressed beats is mainly *light-**HEAVY*** or *ti-**TUM***. This is called *iambic.* So, the *metre*, or rhythm, of the stanza is three lines of *iambic tetrametre* followed by a line of *iambic trimetre.* It is a rhythm that sounds like normal speech.

---

[2] Preface to "*Lyrical Ballads*" (1798) – Longman, London
[3] For a fuller discussion of metre, see the section "*A Note on Metre*" at the end.

This regular rhythm is occasionally varied to put an emphasis on important words or ideas, as here where he focuses our attention on the "**tall larch**" by their door. Elsewhere, he uses *enjambment* and *caesura*[4] in the same way, which is noted in the commentaries.

The *rhyme* is similarly regular, rhyming *abab* throughout, another feature of *ballad metre*.

In **stanza one**, Wordsworth sets the scene of an early spring day which has turned warm, giving an opportunity to take a walk outside. A robin is singing from a nearby deciduous fir tree, the larch, a sign of Spring.

In **stanza two**, Wordsworth responds to these signs of spring as to a *"blessing"*, an unlooked for favour, which gives to their surroundings a *"sense of joy"*. These *"bare trees, and mountains bare"*, he knows, will soon become green again. Notice the repetition of *"bare"*, reversing the position of the adjective for emphasis. This is a rhetorical device called *epanalepsis*.

In **stanza three**, Wordsworth addresses his sister, calling her to leave her daily routine and join him outdoors. Note the repeated use of commands – *"make haste"*, *"resign"*, *"Come forth and feel"* - to convey the urgency of his wish and convince her to indulge in this frivolity. Both Wordsworth and Dorothy took their writing

---

[4] *Enjambment* is where the sense of a line continues onto the next, rather than stopping at the end of the line, and *caesura* is a pause or full stop in the middle of a line.

seriously; it was a task they would have set themselves daily.

In **stanza four**, Wordsworth refers to the unseen child staying with them, renamed *"Edward"*, so she has no excuse there. He also urges her to dress appropriately (*"woodland dress"*) for a walk in the country. Women at this time would have had different dresses for wearing inside the house and outside, and coats as we know them barely existed. He also insists that she leaves her *"book"* behind. It was their custom to bring books when walking and settle down to read them, as part of their work, but they have also been shut up indoors during the long winter with little other than reading to occupy themselves. Today, they are going to give themselves *"to idleness"*.

Stanza five develops this idea. They are going to mark the arrival of spring by throwing aside their daily winter routine of reading and writing and give themselves over to a *"living calendar"* drawn up by nature.

In **stanza six**, the focus of the poem moves to a more general contemplation of the effects of spring. Wordsworth associates the coming Spring with rebirth and "**Love**" Note how he opens this line with a *trochee*, two stressed beats together, rather than an *iamb*, for emphasis:

"**Love now**/ a **u**/ni**ver**/sal **truth**"

This is an ancient connection, where the warming of the earth is mirrored by an upsurge in feelings between people, and between people and the earth itself.

In **stanza seven**, Wordsworth suggests that a single *"moment"* outdoors in this new warmth will tell them more about how they should live their lives than any amount of thinking (*"reason"*). The *"spirit"* of Spring will enter their bodies and show them how to live.

In **stanza eight**, Wordsworth predicts what the long-term effects of this day will be. They will take the feelings (*"temper"*) aroused by this Spring day and live by them for the rest of their lives.

In **stanza nine**, he calls the influence of this Spring day *"the blessed power"*. This is not a reference to the God of any organised religion, but to a spirituality that Wordsworth shared with other Romantics. They believed that there was a universal spirit which united men and the natural world, from which we should learn how to live (*"frame...our souls"*). He believes that *"our souls"* should be in harmony (*"tuned"*) with this spirit, which tells us to *"love"* one another and the natural world.

In **stanza ten**, Wordsworth returns to the here and now, and calls again to his sister to *"Come!"*, the repetition of this command conveying his eagerness to go outside. He repeats his advice given in **stanza four**, bringing the poem to a neat conclusion, ending where it began, with the relationship between the two of them and their relationship with the natural world.

Sunday Dip – John Clare

Context

John Clare (1793-1864) was a contemporary of Wordsworth and, like him, came from a rural background. They shared a love of the natural world and were both close observers of it. However, unlike Wordsworth, Clare was born into poverty and it is probable that early malnutrition affected his physical and mental health throughout his life. Clare received schooling until the age of 12, and then worked as a manual labourer until the 1820s. For a time, he was a gardener at Burghley House near Peterborough, seat of the Marquis of Exeter, who supported him financially in later life. In his later years, Clare suffered from severe mental health problems and was committed to a number of *"asylums"*, hospitals for the mentally sick, including Northampton, where he lived for twenty years and died aged 71.

Clare was inspired to write poetry after buying the collection *"The Seasons"* by 18th century Scottish poet James Thompson. Clare's first book of poetry, *Poems Descriptive of Rural Life and Scenery,* was published in 1820 by John Taylor, who was known to a local bookseller, and who was the publisher of Keats. This volume and the subsequent *Village Minstrel and Other Poems* were well-received, and he was dubbed *"the Northamptonshire Peasant Poet"*. *"Sunday Dip"* is from his middle period, before he was hospitalised.

Themes

The *"merry boys"* in the poem all share a common joy – bathing in a local waterhole on a hot summer's day. Sunday would be special, as it was the only day that working people had as a holiday. The poem is notable for the detailing of the activities the boys share together, which suggests that Clare is recalling his own childhood pleasures, as he was an agricultural labourer whilst still a child, as was common amongst the rural poor. He shares this joy in being outside in the open air with Wordsworth, as evoked in the poem *"To My Sister"*.

Form, structure and language

The poem is a *sonnet,* with fourteen lines of *iambic pentametre*[5] in *rhyming couplets*.[6] The metre is shown here, with the stressed beats indicated in **bold**:

*The **mor**/ning **road**/ is **thronged**/ with **me**/rry **boys**
Who **seek**/ the **wa**/ter **for**/ their **Sun**/day **joys***

The *sonnet* is divided in two, with an *octet* (eight lines), a *volta* at line nine, and a *sestet* (six lines). Clare frequently wrote sonnets and other traditional verse forms. However, he also uses non-standard, or dialect, words and grammar, reflecting the sound of the speech of Northamptonshire, although this poem is mostly in standard English. Like Wordsworth, he uses the

---

[5] Five stressed beats with the pattern *light-**heavy*** or ti-**TUM**
[6] Pairs of rhyming lines

rhythms of speech and the language is simple and unadorned.

Each *couplet* uses *full rhymes* [7] and is self-contained, with an *end-stop*[8] on the second line and tells a little part of the story of the boys *Sunday Dip*.

In the **opening couplet** Clare watches, or recalls, the boys congregating to enjoy the simple pleasures offered to them by a swim in a local pond.

The **second couplet** shows them racing to the water and paddling at the margin. Clare uses the *enjambment*[9] from *"wade/and dance"* to lead us into the water with them.

The **third couplet** focuses on the ringleader, the first of the boys to go in deeper, followed by others who go into the water up *"to the chin"*. It is possible that the boys cannot swim, as this was a time before swimming was taught in schools and there would have been no need for an ordinary working boy to learn, living inland, with little leisure time and with little chance of visiting the seaside.

The **fourth couplet** confirms that being in deep water is unfamiliar, as they have to *"lose their fears"*, as they

---

[7] A *full rhyme* is also called a *perfect rhyme*, as in *"boys/joys"* or *"wade/shade"*.

[8] *End-stop*ping is where the sense of the line ends at the end of the line. It is the opposite of *enjambment*, where the sense of the line runs over the line and onto the next.

[9] *Enjambment* is where the sense of the line runs over the line and onto the next.

play about in the water, ducking under and laughing as the water rushes over their ears.

The **fifth couplet**, at line 9, marks the *volta* of the sonnet, where the argument or story changes direction or subject. Perhaps growing tired of just splashing about, they devise a crude boat from the bull-*rushes* (tall water plants), clamber on and try to float across the deeper water – again suggesting they cannot swim.

In the **sixth couplet,** they manage to float under the surrounding willow trees (willow trees commonly grow by water) although the raft is in danger of sinking. Clare's use of local dialect is evident here. In modern Received Pronunciation, "*stoop*" and "*up*" would not be a *full rhyme*, but in Northampton dialect, "*up*" would be pronounced closer to "*oop*".

In the **final couplet**, the attention turns to those not on the raft ("*the others*") who float away unaided by the rushes (or possibly the other boys?) and happily continue playing in the water. The "*half the day*" shows how precious, and how rare, this opportunity is for the boys, only children still, but with the burden of six-day-a-week working already clouding their lives.

Mild the mist upon the hill – Emily Bronte

Context

To understand Emily Bronte's prose and poetry, you need to understand the circumstances of her short, and arguably tragic life. Emily had five siblings – two sisters who died, aged 10 and 12, of consumption (what we now know as tuberculosis, a chronic lung disease which was incurable at the time) while away at boarding school; a brother, Branwell, who eventually died of drink and drugs aged 31; Anne, who also died of consumption aged 28, shortly after her brother's death, and Charlotte, author of *"Jane Eyre"*, who was the only one to marry, but died in childbirth in 1855, aged 39. Emily died in 1848, the same year as Anne, aged 30.

For much of their short lives the children lived in relative isolation high on the Yorkshire Moors in the parsonage of the village of Haworth, where their father was the parson. Their mother died when they were very young and they were brought up by their aunt, who was a strict Methodist. Her life was characterised by self-improvement, religiosity and study. Branwell was educated at home, but the four girls attended school for a time and, for the standards of the day, were well-read. In childhood, Emily and Charlotte were left to their own resources for entertainment and amused themselves by chronicling the events of two imaginary countries – Gondal and Angria – writing the stories and poems in tiny, handmade booklets. The young women hoped to make a living by teaching and were for a time governesses and tutors; Charlotte and Emily lived briefly in France learning French. However, their dreams of starting their own school in England came to nothing. When Mr Bronte's eyesight began to fail and their brother, Branwell, sank into despair, drugs and drink following a scandalous affair with the wife of his employer, the girls became largely confined to Haworth.

This poem was written in 1839, just after Emily returned home from a period spent teaching in Halifax, which ruined her fragile health. It is intensely melancholy and reflects both her homesickness and her ill health, as well as some ambivalence about returning to her childhood home.

Themes

Emily Bronte is variously described by biographers and critics as "spiritual" and "visionary", as well as highly imaginative. The landscape of the Moors infuses Emily's writings, most notably in her masterpiece, the novel *"Wuthering Heights"*. The scene she describes in the poem is the wild Yorkshire moorland that loomed over the parsonage and to which she was drawn, finding in it both inspiration and solace, as well as memory. There is a strong feeling of **belonging to a place** in most of Bronte's poems, as in this one. With Wordsworth, she shares a close affinity with the natural world. The poem is also intensely **melancholy**, although the incident about which she writes suggests that she should be feeling more positive, as she is speaking about the aftermath of a storm, when the rain has stopped, and fine weather seems promised. The tone suggests ambivalent feelings about her home at this point in her life.

Form, structure and language

The poem is strangely contradictory in its effect and its message. On the one hand, it opens by telling us that it is NOT going to storm in the morning as the *"mist"* is *"mild"*, which promises fine weather. And yet, the overall tone is of a leaden sorrow, both now and in the past, as she remembers her childhood. This is due, not only to the use of *pathetic fallacy*[10], but also the *metre*.

The poem is another, like *"To My Sister"*, written in *ballad form*, with lines of *tetrametre* and *trimetre* and a regular *abab* rhyme scheme. However, the pattern of stressed and unstressed beats is more varied than in Wordsworth's poem, the first stanza being mainly in *trochees*, **HEAVY**-*light* or **TUM**-*ti*, rather than *iambs*. This gives the poem a slower, more ponderous tone, to evoke the feelings of sorrow which fill the poem:

***"Mild** the/ **mist** up/**on** the /**hill**,*
***Tel**ling/ **not** of /**storms** to/**morrow**"*

This also places emphasis on the *alliterated "mild/mist"* softening the line, like the softness of the weather. Then the stress falls on *"Tell/not/storms/"* which should give a positive feeling – but the heaviness of the stress suggests the opposite, as if the speaker is weighed down with *"sorrow"*.

---

[10] *Pathetic fallacy* (literally "false feeling") is the use of landscape or weather to mirror human emotions. It is similar to, but not the same as, *personification*.

In the **first stanza**, Bronte looks out across the Moors to which she has returned. The day has been stormy, but it is now calm, and the *"mild...mist"* suggests that it is going to be fine *"to-morrow"*. She uses *pathetic fallacy*, equating the rain that has fallen with the skies weeping overflowing tears, which have now ceased.

In **stanza two**, she remembers her childhood at the parsonage in Haworth surrounded by these Moors. The exclamatory *"Oh, ..."* is an expression of her longing for those *"days of youth"*. She recalls her childhood home and the *"hall door"* that opened on to a vista of the hills. Notice how she links **stanzas two and three** using *enjambment* on *"door/I watch"*, leading us to view the *"cloudy evening "* alongside her, as she stands at the open door.

Stanza three describes this summer evening of her youth, which is similar to the one she is experiencing now. *"After a day of rain"* the mist is blue and soft and covers the distant hills, signalling fine weather. But the word *"pall"* adds to the tone of sorrow. A *"pall"* is the covering placed over a corpse – inferring that these childhood days are also dead.

Stanza four returns to the present. The earlier rain, which Bronte likens again to *"tears"*, still lies on the long grass. The smell of the garden after rain again reminds her of her childhood – the *"other years"*. This circular structure suggests that she is trapped at Haworth, unable to move forward and constantly pulled back to her childhood home.

Captain Cook (To My Brother) – Letitia Elizabeth Landon

Context

Letitia Elizabeth Landon (1802-1838), or L.E.L. as she was known, was a precocious child of wealthy parents who was educated from the age of five at a prestigious London school. She was then privately tutored at home, where it was claimed that she knew more than her tutor. She started writing poetry at an early age and published her first poem at 18. Two volumes of poetry soon followed, as well as regular poems in the weekly literary magazine the *Literary Gazette*, (at which she was now chief reviewer), signing them "L.E.L". This created excited speculation as to the identity of the poet amongst literary circles and she was considered one of the most important poets of her time, read by the Brontes and referenced by George Eliot in *"Middlemarch"*.

Her early adult life was surrounded by rumours of scandalous sexual behaviour and illegitimate children by her publisher and agent, William Jerdan. This resulted in the ending of an engagement to John Foster, a friend of Charles Dickens. Landon later married the Governor of the Gold Coast (now Guyana) to where she emigrated, dying shortly after arriving, at the age of 36, after drinking poison, either by accident or as suicide.

In the early 20th century, her reputation declined. She was derided by Virginia Woolf, who has a character in one of her novels, "*Orlando*", pour ink over her verses, and largely forgotten. Like many other Victorian female poets, Landon's work has been largely neglected until recently.[11] It is also not very good, which may contribute to its obscurity.

Whittington Henry was Landon's younger brother by only two years, but when he went to university, she supported him through her earnings from her poetry and writing for the *Gazette*. It appears, however, that Whittington, who became a clergyman and eventually Dean of Exeter, repaid his sisters' generosity in later years by spreading the rumours about her love-affairs and possible suicide.

The poem dwells on Landon's and her brother Whittington's creation of a fictitious world based on their shared reading of the life of Captain James Cook, the explorer and navigator who charted both Newfoundland and the Southern Pacific (the "*Fair South Seas*"). He was the first European to chart the east coast of Australia and to circumnavigate New Zealand. He was killed in 1779 in Hawaii by the indigenous people during a failed attempt to take the Chief hostage in return for a stolen boat.

---

[11] A new biography of Landon was published in May 2019. An interesting review can be found here:
https://www.theguardian.com/books/2019/may/24/lel-by-lucasta-miller-review-poet-letitia-elizabeth-landon

Themes

The dedication of the poem to her brother, like Wordsworth's to his sister, suggests a strong childhood bond between brother and sister, created by their shared experiences. Although they no longer talk of these childhood fantasies, she recalls them fondly, and the home that they shared, and regrets that they have been left behind along with their childhood. As in Bronte's poem, **childhood is a place which creates strong feelings of belonging** and one to which you can return in memory, recapturing those youthful feelings. Similarly, **memory** enables the Island Man and the Emigrée to recall their lost homelands.

Form, structure and language

The poem is characterised by the long lines of *iambic hexametre* or *alexandrines* – lines with six stressed beats in a pattern *ti-**TUM***.

The lines are usually broken in half, by the use of a *caesura*[12]:

"*From **whence**/ we **took**/ our **fut**ure,// to **fa**/shion **as**/we **might**"*

This creates a sing-song rhythm, which is not always effective when the sense of the line does not easily break in the middle of the line:

"*When the pulse danced those light measures that again it cannot know!*"

---

[12] A *caesura* is a break or pause in the middle of a line.

This is very clumsy, both rhythmically and syntactically[13].

At times, the lines end on an awkward stress which feels unnatural:

"All **o/**ther **fav/**ourite **he**roes// were **no/**thing **be/**side **him**"

Each *quatrain* (four-line) stanza has a regular rhyme scheme *aabb,* which Landon finds difficult to maintain. She is forced to twist the *syntax* to make the rhymes fit:

"*As actual, but more pleasant, than what the day now brings*"

which is an ugly construction.

The **first stanza** is addressed to her brother, now an adult, the "*you*" of the first line. She asks if he can remember their childhood when they made up stories ("*fancies*") which excited their imaginations ("*pulse danced*"). They no longer talk of these stories of long ago ("*yore*"), as they have both grown up - and possibly apart.

The **second stanza** recalls them reading books, the source of the make-believe, into which they inserted

---

[13] *Syntax* means the arrangement of words in a sentence. In English, word order in a sentence determines meaning, as in "the cat sat on the mat" rather than "the mat sat on the cat", which are the same words be in a different order and, as a result, have a totally different (and nonsensical) meaning. Poor *syntax* can, therefore, make meaning obscure.

themselves as the heroine and hero. The last line suggests (although it is muddled) that this make-believe world was more real, and *"more pleasant"* than their lives now.

Stanza three opens with setting the scene of a summer's evening when her brother brings home a particular book– an account of the Voyages of Captain Cook (the *"he"* of the line), famous for exploring the southern Pacific Ocean. The brother and sister are captivated, reading on until dusk falls.

Stanza four tells how they re-enacted Cook's adventures, imagining the pond to be the sea he sailed and the waterlilies the Pacific islands. *"Morning smile"* is odd. At first, it reads as if it is the water lilies smiling, with *"smile"* as a verb. But taken with the next line, *"morning smile"* must be a *metaphor* for daybreak, with *"smile"* as a noun.

Stanza five has equally awkward syntax across the first two lines. She is stating that no one could be luckier, in the lottery that is life, than a sailor, who has drawn the golden ticket. The life of a sailor seemed to the children to be the best that life could offer, as they imagine themselves sailing the seas and discovering new lands. The *"storm and strife"* seems to refer to their real lives, rather than the sailors', suggesting that the make-believe was an escape from the world around them.

Stanza six confirms this idea with the reference to the *"lonely"* garden, where they were left to create their own amusement. But their play took them to other lands and opened up new possibilities. Her regret at the passing of this happy time is contained in the exclamation *"Ah!"*, as the real world closes in around them as they grow up and they can no longer enter this land of make-believe.

Stanza seven laments the loss of the garden in which they played out their fantasies. The first two lines emphasise the absence of the familiar place, with *"not"* and *"single"* and the balancing of *"ploughed"* and *"cut down"* in the two halves of the *alexandrine*. The last two lines of the stanza ask a rhetorical question *"Where..."* have the flowers and trees of this garden gone? How precious they seem to her is shown by the use of the descriptors *"silver"* for the Guelder flowers and *"gold"* for the yellow flowers of the laburnum tree, which are brought as an offering to the Spring.[14]. The naming of particular plants also suggests that they were special to her.

The **final stanza** answers her question. All these things have *"vanished"* like the childhood of the children that played among them. The idea of preciousness is repeated with the word *"treasures"*. Their adult lives take place in a *"darker"* place. However, the name of Captain Cook still resonates with her, bringing back fond memories of the games they played, enjoying the

---

[14] *Guelder roses* are not roses but a species of *viburnum*, a small, flowering shrub which has large heads of white flowers. A *laburnum* is a small ornamental tree that has long racemes of flowers that hang down, giving it the alternate name of "golden rain".

vicarious thrill of the dangers he faced in his explorations and feeling sad when he dies.

Clear and Gentle Stream – Robert Bridges

Context

Robert Seymour Bridges (1844-1930) trained as a doctor and worked in hospitals, including Bartholomew's, London, until 1882 when he suffered ill-health and retired. He wrote poetry and prose throughout his life and was Poet Laureate from 1913 until his death. This poem, which is titled *"Elegy,"* was written in 1873 and is the first poem in the collection *"Shorter Poems"* published in 1890.

Themes

Bridges looks back upon his childhood and recalls happier times, as do Clare, Bronte and Landon. As in Clare's and Bronte's poems, the setting is *particularised* – they describe places which are important to them, not just any pool, hill or garden. Clare describes a swimming hole which was the scene for many happy Sundays, which he recalls fondly. Bronte looks out upon the familiar hills of the Yorkshire Dales surrounding Haworth and recalls the child peering out of the door at those same hills. Landon remembers the plants in the garden. The stream Bridges describes is not any stream, but one which Bridges knew well in his childhood and to which he has returned. In all four poems, the poets convey a sense of belonging in the past, in their **childhoods, which are rooted in a place,** from which adulthood has torn them away. Themes of being **uprooted from a place where you belong** recur in *"The Emigrée"* and *"Island Man"*. *"The Emigrée"* was uprooted as child and remembers her city in terms of *"sunlight"*, whilst the Island Man recalls his *"emerald"* isle through the sounds and sights of nature.

Form, structure and language

An *"Elegy"* has come to mean a lament for the dead, although it originally had a broader meaning. Samuel Taylor Coleridge, a poet-friend of Wordsworth, described it: *"Elegy presents every thing as lost and gone or absent and future."* Elegies are serious, personal and thoughtful, as is the case with this poem, where Bridges mourns the loss of his childhood.

The poem is in four, twelve-line stanzas of *trochaic trimetres* – lines with three stressed beats in a pattern **HEAVY**-*light* or **Tum**-*ti*. These lines are *catalectic* – they are missing the final unstressed syllable, ending on a stress:

*"**Calm** and **gen**tle **stream**!*
***Known** and **loved** so **long**,*

This gives the poem a heavy, melancholy tone, in keeping with the *elegaic* form.

The rhyme scheme is the same in each stanza – *abba/cdcd/eeff*, - which might suggest that the stanza breaks down into three self-contained sections of four lines, with the sense following the rhyme scheme. However, Bridges runs on lines 4 to 5 in each stanza, which gives the stanza more flow, like the stream he is describing:

> "*And the idle dream*   line 4
> *Of my boyish day;*"   line 5

The effect of further variations in the rhyme scheme are noted in the commentaries on the stanzas.

The stream can be regarded as a *metaphor* for Life flowing past him. In youth, Bridges was optimistic and hopeful; now he is aging and looks back on wasted opportunities and lost dreams.

In **stanza one**, Bridges returns to the stream he knew in his childhood and addresses it directly, indicated by the exclamation mark.[15] The stream was the boy's confidant – he told it what he was feeling and hoping for the future (*"song"*, *"idle dream"*). On his return, these same feelings and thoughts haunt him, but the boy's cheerful *"song"* is now a sad *"lament"* and his *"dream"* has come to nothing (*"idle"*).

In **stanza two**, he sits in the place where he sat as a boy, where the trees arch over the water creating a roof (*"eaves"*). Notice how again Bridges runs lines 4 and 5 of the stanza together, using *enjambment*. A further use of *enjambment* to continue the flow of the lines is found between lines 6 and 7: *"play/Shipwreck"*. The word *"shipwreck"* recalls his childhood games where he imagined sailing on the high seas. The stanza ends with

---

[15] This is called *"apostrophe"* in rhetoric where the speaker addresses a third party, here the stream rather than the reader.

an image of calm, with the swans serenely passing and the fish motionless in the water, as if he has briefly recaptured the contentment of his childhood and the troubles of old age have been laid aside.

Stanza three continues with his reminiscences of childhood, spending lazy afternoons by the stream until evening falls, signalled by the bell tolling in a nearby church. The approach of evening is *personified* as a woman *"creeping"* towards him, bringing the shadows, but also the bright lamp of the moon. Again, the stanza ends on a note of peace, although with a note of impending darkness as night, and thoughts of old age, return.

In the **final stanza**, he once again addresses the stream, as he prepares to leave it. The negative of *"does not flow"* suggests that where he lives now is a less pleasant place and he is reluctant to leave. Extending the *metaphor*, it also means that his life-force is ebbing as he grows old. He feels that the stream should hear his childhood *"song"* once again as in his boyhood, as he no longer sings it. He urges the stream to be satisfied, as he is, to express his hopes and dreams once more in this place as he used to, even if this youthful promise has come to nothing.

I Remember, I Remember

Context

Thomas Hood (1799-1845) is known today for a few memorable poems, of which *"I Remember..."* is one. Another is the punning verse on *"November"* which begins (and continues similarly):

"No sun – no moon!
No morn – no noon –
No dawn – no dusk – no proper time of day."

And ends: *"November!"*

Hood was born in Cheapside in London, in the heart of the city, above his father's bookshop. At the age of 12, he moved to Islington, a more rural part of London at the time. Even so, details in the poem suggest that the landscape depicted by Hood in the poem is imaginary, rather than based on his own childhood experiences – as does the presence of a fictitious *"brother"* in stanza two.

Hood wrote for a number of popular magazines of his time and edited *"The London Gazette"*. He was friends with, amongst others, Charles Dickens, and his later poems, including *"Song of the Shirt"*, were concerned with the plight of the poor. This poem dates from 1826 and was first published in *"Friendship's Offering: A literary album"*.

Hood was never in robust health and died aged 45.

Themes

In common with the preceding poem in the collection, *"Clear and Gentle Stream"*, the poem looks back on a happy childhood from the vantage point of older age and disappointment. As noted, it is probably based less on an actual childhood memory than those recalled by Landon, Bronte or Clare. However, like those poems, it mourns a lost world of childhood, and equates childhood with a place from which the poet has been expelled, as if from the Garden of Eden, which his description of his childhood home recalls. Similarly, Rumens recalls her *"sunlight-clear"* city where she lived as a child, to which there is *"no way back"*.

Form, structure and language

Each eight-line stanza is in *common metre* – alternating lines of *iambic tetrametre* and *iambic trimetre*. Like Wordsworth's use of the closely related *ballad metre*, this rhythm evokes childhood nursey rhymes and songs, such as *"Sing a Song of Sixpence"*, in keeping with his theme of returning to his past. The rhyme scheme is also similar, each *quatrain*[16] rhyming *abcb*.

Each of the four stanzas moves from a memory of childhood happiness to a darker present where he is a man – from day to night, from flowers of *"light"* to a hint of death, from being carefree to being burdened with care, from reaching to heaven to being weighed down with sin.

---

[16] A *quatrain* is four lines

In **stanza one**, he opens with his recurring refrain "*I Remember, I remember*", the use of *anaphora*[17] giving emphasis to the power of memory, and a note of longing for days long past. He recalls the house in simple, childlike language: "*little*", "*peeping*", "*wink*". Back then, the days were just the right length, neither too short nor too long. Now, he wishes that the night had brought death.

In **stanza two**, he moves out of the house into the surrounding garden full of flowers. The description of the flowers is generalised, with none of the particular detail that characterises, for example, Bridges' memories, such as the leaves playing "*shipwreck*", or Landon's water-lily "*islands*" in the pond. Even the roses are a bland "*red and white*". By "*lily-cups*" he probably means waterlilies. He uses the shortened form of violets ("*vi'lets*") to ensure the word is pronounced as two rather than three syllables, for the scansion[18] of the line. The flowers seem radiant, reflecting the sun that has come "*peeping*" in his window. He recalls the lilac tree where a robin built its nest and the laburnum[19] that his brother planted, and which is still growing. The hyphenating of the line "*– The tree is living yet*" may suggest that the brother, however, has died, adding to his sorrow.

In **stanza three**, Hood recalls the swing in the garden. Whereas most of the lines of the poem are *end-stopped*[20],

---

[17] *Anaphora* means repetition at the beginning of a clause
[18] "*scansion*" means the rhythmic pattern or metre
[19] See Landon's poem

he uses *enjambment* to convey the upward rush of the swing to meet the *"swallows"* with whom he shares the air: *"must rush as fresh/To swallows on the wing"*. He follows up the idea of sharing the air with the swallows, by saying that his *"spirit"*, his mood, was as light as a feather *"then"*, when he was a child, but is now *"heavy"*. He also laments that even bathing in pools, as he did in summer, would now be unable to *"cool"* the heat of the sickness (*"fever"*) which consumes him.

In **the last stanza**, he uses the memory of the tall, dark green *"fir trees"*, reaching to the sky as a *metaphor* for the child being closer to God than the Man. *"Fir trees"* are evergreens with a columnar, or pencil, shape. From the child's perceptive, they seem to almost touch the sky, their reaching conveyed by the *enjambment* between *"slender tops/Were close…"* The Man, older and wiser, knows that this was childish fantasy, but it brings him *"little joy"*, as he is tainted with the sins of the world and is further away from heaven than he was as an *"ignorant"* child.

The description of the garden, the references to the *"spirit"* and the reaching for heaven, give the poem a spiritual or religious overtone, equating the loss of childhood with a Fall from Grace.

---

[20] *"end-stopping"* is where the sense of the line ends at the end of the line, often with punctuation

Island Man– Grace Nichols

Context

Grace Nichols was born in 1960 in British Guiana, now Guyana, part of the Guianas, a region on the north coast of South America. Nichols emigrated to England in the 1970s and is the partner of fellow Guyanese poet John Agard.

The "Island" of the poem is one of the islands in the Caribbean Sea which forms the seaboard of Guyana. It was first published in the volume *"The Fat Black Woman's Poems"* in 1984.

Themes

The poem is an imaginative recreation of the thoughts and feelings of a Caribbean immigrant living in London and contrasts the sights and sounds of his home with the sights and sounds of where he now lives. **It explores the immigrant experience, and what "belonging" to the place where you were born means to someone who has been "dislocated"** and moved to another country. This theme is also explored by Choman Hardi in *"My Mother's Kitchen"*, and, like the Island Man, it is the natural features of her lost home that the mother mourns - the vine *"that spread over the trellis"*. Carol Rumens in *"The Emigrée"* misses the *"sunlight"* which bathed the lost city of her childhood. These **feelings of loss** are shared with Clare, Landon, Bronte and Bridges who similarly find themselves drawn back in memory to an earlier place and time.

Form, structure and language

Unlike the poems of other poets in this collection who explore the immigrant experience, this poem is written in the third person, although Nichols is herself an immigrant. She enters imaginatively into the man's experience, drawing on her own feelings about having left the country of her birth.

The poem is in *free verse*, with no regular rhythm nor rhyme scheme. It is in four loosely-structured stanzas. In the first, the man wakes up; the second recalls the sounds and sights of his island home, of which he has been dreaming; the third brings him back to London; in the fourth, the man *"heaves"* himself out of bed.

Nichols makes extensive use of the sounds of words to mimic the sounds that the Island Man remembers from his home and hears around him now in London, and to convey the confusion the man feels as he awakes from a dream of his Island Home to the reality of his new life in London.

The lack of punctuation also shows how the two lives merge, images of the Island life running into those of London almost imperceptibly.

Stanza one opens with the single declarative *"Morning"*, placing us in the scene, as does Blakemore in *"Peckham Rye Lane"*, which opens *"The sun, today -"*. The man awakes still hearing *"in his head"* the sounds of his dream – the *"blue surf"* breaking on the beaches of his Caribbean island. Nichols uses the *sibilance*[21] of "*sound/surf/steady*" to imitate the sound of waves on the sand. "*Wombing*", an image of motherhood, suggests that the sea is life-giving.

In **stanza two**, some of his dream-images are described, images of life and light and energy – the "*wild seabirds*", the fishermen "*pushing*" their boats out to sea and the sun that comes up strongly every day ("*Defiantly*"). This imagery can be compared with Rumen's descriptions of her "*sunlight-clear*" city. Nichols's uses further *sibilance* with "*seabirds/fisher/push/sea/ sun/surfacing*" echoing the sounds of the sea.

His Island is "*green*" and fertile (linking back to "*wombing*") and how precious it is to him is suggested by the use of the *metaphoric* "*emerald*", a precious gem. The last line, which tells how he always has to "*come back*" to reality as he wakes up, is linked *typographically*[22] to the next stanza by the aside of "*groggily, groggily*" to describe his confusion – half-asleep, half-awake – just as the words are printed half-way between the two stanzas.

In *stanza three*, the man is still caught between the two places he inhabits – the Island of his birth and of his dreams, and the London where he lives. The man confuses the sounds of the sea in his dream with those of the London traffic outside. He "*Comes back to sands*" which logically should be "sounds", and to the

---

[21] *Sibilance* is repeated "*s*" and "*sh*" sounds.
[22] See the section "*About this Guide*" for an explanation of *typography* –the way the words are printed on the page.

"*soar*", which should be "roar", of the traffic outside. "*Surge*" unites the two, the sea-sounds giving way to "*wheels*" on tarmac and the roar of the North Circular Road, that orbits the city

Notice that, in this stanza, the bright "*blue*" and "*green*" of the Island give way to "*grey*", and images of life – sea, birds, greenery – give way to the dead metal of passing cars ("*metallic*"). Now the *sibilance* of "*sands/soar/surge*" imitates the sound of tyres on tarmac.

In **the last stanza**, the man tries to block out these alien sounds by putting his pillow over his head, "*muffling*" them. He almost recaptures his dream, indicated by the "pillow **waves**" which suggest he is pulled back to the sounds of the sea on his island. But it is only momentary. He has to face reality.

The final line, "*Another London day*", is set apart from the preceding stanza, as he "*heaves himself*" out of bed, like a wave breaking on this alien shore.

Peckham Rye Lane – Amy (A.K.) Blakemore

Context

Amy (now published as A.K.) Blakemore was born in 1991 in Deptford, South London, close to where this poem is set. It was written in 2007 when she was sixteen and studying at the local comprehensive school. She began writing poetry in response to a challenge from her English teacher to write better than Carol Ann Duffy, then the Poet Laureate, who is widely studied at GCSE, and whom she disliked. By the time she went up to St Edmund Hall, Oxford, to study English, she had already won the Foyle's Young Poet award in both 2007 and 2008 and published her first pamphlet of poems before she took Finals in 2012.

Peckham S.E.15 is the heart of the Nigerian diaspora in London, described by *Timeout* as *"the beating heart of Little Lagos"*.[23] Rye Lane is a busy market street with a vast range of food stalls and traders.

Themes

The poem is a homage[24] to her home, South East London, and captures the multi-cultural aspects of this diverse part of the capital city. As in Nichols' *"Island Man"*, the use of detail evokes a particular, and familiar,

---

[23] The full article can be read here: https://www.timeout.com/london/blog/12-reasons-to-go-to-peckham-rye-rye-lane-se15-042216
[24] A *homage* is writing which praises and pays respects to the subject.

place. However, unlike many poets in this collection, Blakemore still belongs to the community she celebrates, and the poem ends on a note of contentment. It can be compared to the final view of the city in *"The Emigrée"*, where in spite of being exiled from her city, and the forces of darkness that have invaded it, it still exists in her heart and mind as *"sunlight"*.

Form, structure and language

The poem is in *free verse* with no regular rhythm or rhyme scheme. Rather than being laid out in defined stanzas, much use is made of the *typography*, as in *"Island Man"*, where the layout on the page is part of the poem.

As in *"Island Man"*, the poem opens with a declarative *"The sun, today – "* setting the poem at a particular time on a particular day. *"Leaks desperation"* is a form of *hypallage* or a *transferred epithet*. It is not the sun that *"leaks"* but the people it is shining on. Not only is the sun trying hard to shine brightly, perhaps through London pollution, but the people on which it is shining are sweating uncomfortably in the unfamiliar heat (*"leaks"*). *"Desperation"* is also a possible allusion to the comment by the American writer Henry Thoreau that *"The mass of men lead lives of quiet desperation"*, which is supported by both the rhyme with *"perspiration"* and the later reference to William Blake, the poet and social commentator.

The sweat is described as *"gunmetal drops"*, suggesting both a grimy sheen and also a hard, unforgiving quality.

These drops of sweat *"gather"*, the word set alone on a separated line, as if the images of the previous lines come together on this one word.

The poet is travelling to Peckham. The reference to *"Primark"*, a low cost clothing store, as indicated by the *"£2"* price-tags, pinpoints that this is a less affluent part of the city. The clothes in the store are likened to sea creatures washed up on the shore, lying limply (*"flaccid"*). They are in soft, pastel colours – the pink of the hanging *"tentacles"* of a jellyfish or the *"mauve"* said to be liked by older women – creating a *"rainbow"* of colour on the racks, the *metaphor* a possible reference to *"rainbow nation"*, reflecting the multi-cultural community which surrounds the store.

Blakemore describes the tight-packed crowds on the market street in an image of a *"coconut shell"*, a solid mass on the outside and packed with flesh on the inside. It also references a popular food of the people of the area.

The diversity of the area is captured by listing the wares for sale. Blakemore uses a series of *internal* and *eye-rhymes*[25] to emphasise the variety: *"combs/ phones/ cornrows/cornflower"*. The confusion of colour and ethnicities is also conveyed by the contrasting hairstyles seen: one with *"cornrows"*, hair tightly curled to the head; one with a blue scrunchie, like the *"cornflower"* of

---

[25] An *internal rhyme* is one where the rhyme occurs in the middle of a line; an *eye-rhyme* is where words look like they rhyme but do not.

the English countryside, and another with their black hair (*"liquorice"*) woven into patterns.

The scene then shifts to a takeaway restaurant on the street[26], KFC, famous for its *"finger-lickin' good"* fried chicken. Inside, she can see babies and children tucking into their meals, fretful and angry, captured humorously by the image of them holding their chicken drumsticks like *"weapons"*, with which to berate their frazzled parents. Note the *alliteration* in the line on *"wailing"* and *"weapons"*, that creates the humour. The reference to *"plaid-dressed"* is obscure, although it may suggest further cultural diversity, as *"plaid"* is a popular clothing pattern for middle-class white children.

The pavement outside is covered with unidentifiable litter and dropped food (*"gruesome meat"*). Blakemore imagines the pavement as the base of a hairbrush on which the throngs of people stand upright like the *"bristles"*, suggesting both their closeness one to another but also their individuality.

The **final four lines**, deliberately separated one from another for dramatic effect, reference William Blake, the late eighteenth century poet, engraver and social commentator on the plight of the poor in London, of which he too was a citizen. His poem *"London"* denounced the treatment of the poor by both Church and State. Blakemore imagines the Angels, that Blake depicted in some of his engravings, gazing down with him on the crowds below, bathing them in a benign

---

[26] There is one on the Lane – no. 32-36.

radiance. The separated lines give significance to the words. This is a scene of humankind thronging the streets of London with which he would have been familiar, and which he loved.

Ultimately, Blakemore presents this part of London as a positive life-force, blessed by the ghosts of its past. In spite of its outward appearance as a sweaty, crowded, smelly chaos, it is a celebration of the diversity of life in this part of this great City that is her home.

We Refugees – Benjamin Zephaniah

Context

Benjamin Zephaniah was born in Birmingham to parents from the Caribbean. He describes himself as *"Poet, writer, lyricist, musician and naughty boy."* He has recently (May 2018) published his autobiography. Zephaniah has a blog which gives details of his life that can be found here: https://benjaminzephaniah.com.

According to the United Nations:

"Refugees are persons fleeing armed conflict or persecution. There were 21.3 million of them worldwide at the end of 2015. Their situation is often so perilous and intolerable that they cross national borders to seek safety in nearby countries, and thus become internationally recognized as "refugees" with access to assistance from States, UNHCR, and other organizations. They are so recognized precisely because it is too dangerous for them to return home, and they need sanctuary elsewhere. These are people for whom denial of asylum has potentially deadly consequences". (UNHCR)

Zephaniah wrote the poem in 2000 and it was included in his collection *"Wicked World"*, when the current worldwide refugee crisis was just starting. It seems even more relevant in 2019, as Europe grapples with the influx of refugees from the multiple ideological conflicts in Africa and the Middle East, and the USA closes its borders to those fleeing violence fuelled by political and economic tensions in Central America.

Themes

Whereas Blakemore writes about a place which she clearly sees as still being "home", Nichols, Rumens and Zephaniah **put themselves in the shoes of people who have no "home"** but find themselves displaced and wandering.

Zephaniah turns his attention to the plight of Refugees, fleeing the lands of their birth and trying to find new homes in countries that may be reluctant to accept them. He warns that anyone can become a refugee, forced from their homes by changes in political regimes, by climate change or by societal pressures. None of us are immune. After all, we all started out as refugees - from Africa, where the human race began.

Form, structure and language

Zephaniah is also a dub performance artist, which relies on regular rhythm for effect. This poem is written mainly in loose *iambic trimetre* and *iambic tetrametre* – lines with three or four stressed beats in a predominantly *ti-**TUM*** pattern. There is no regular rhyme scheme.

The poem is structured as two groups of five stanzas. In each of the two groups, the first four stanzas explore the experience of a refugee from a country undergoing turmoil, in which sections of the population are pitted one against the other. It is tempting to try and put a name to the countries to which he refers, and whilst this may be possible, Zephaniah is using the individual experiences as representative of a worldwide tragedy. The fifth stanza in each group delivers a warning to us all.

The **first four stanzas** of each group are in the first person narrative voice, with Zephaniah adopting the *persona* of the refugees, who tell their tales, opening with the repeated "*I come from…*". Each stanza begins with a positive image of their homeland and ends with the bitter change that has led to their exile.

In **stanza one**, the refugee comes from a "*musical place*" where now music is banned and there is civil war – brother against brother. The language is brutal – "*shoot/tortured*". This, and the following two stanzas, are likely to be a reference to the aftermath of the Afghan Civil War (1992-96) which resulted in the establishment of the Islamic Emirate of Afghanistan and the fundamentalist terrorist organisation of Al-Qaeda.

In **stanza two**, the lost homeland was "*beautiful*", but divided by ethnicity ("*shade of skin*") and religion, and imposed censorship on writers.

In **stanza three**, the "*beautiful place*" bans girls from going to school, suppresses freedom of religion and forces men to grow beards.

Stanza four shifts from homelessness as a result of ethnicity and religion to deforestation, as in the Amazon basin where the clearing of the forest for agriculture ("*forest/field*") has displaced the indigenous Amerindians.

In **stanza five**, the narrative voice changes to Zephaniah's own as he warns that *"we can all be refugees"*, citing how little it takes to make a homeland no longer *"safe"*. A social, political or environmental change can make people strangers in their own homes. Each of us is vulnerable to the *"hate"* of another individual or group.

In **stanza six**, Zephaniah may be using his own thoughts and feelings as the child of immigrants from the Caribbean, in the references to floods and hurricanes. His parents were from Barbados and Jamaica, part of the *"Windrush generation"* who came to England in the 1950s to make up for the shortage of labour in post-war Britain.

Stanza seven suggests that the place of his family's birth is dangerous, and although he wants to *"go there"*, he also wants to survive. Because of this, he too is a "refugee".

In **stanza eight**, this "danger" is explained. His *"place"* is a tourist destination, where, ironically, tourists go to get a tan, their skin colour becoming brown, for which others are persecuted. it is also a place where there is gun-running; he cannot *"tell the price"*, perhaps because he is not there, but also because the price is the cost of human lives.

In **stanza nine,** he seems to speak for all refugees, the homeless and stateless who will be erased from history, losing even their name.

Stanza ten repeats the warning in **stanza five,** that with a change of circumstances we too could become "refugees". It takes very little –an agreement signed with a handshake or a piece of paper and we could end up on the wrong side of the divide. He reminds us that all of us have moved to where we live from somewhere else, a reference to Man coming "out of Africa", and that the move was a *"struggle"* – we are all in the same boat. He asks rhetorically why, having survived the effort of moving to a new place, millennia ago, we cannot be left alone? Why are we still subjected to further disruption from the climate or conflict? Why have we not learnt that we are all refugees?

US – Zaffar Kunial

Context

Zaffar Kunial is a British poet born in Birmingham to an English mother and Nepalese father. The poem is from his first published collection of poetry, "*Us*", which was short-listed for the prestigious TS Eliot Poetry Prize in 2018. Kunial's poetry considers issues of identity, belonging and separation.

Themes

The title is ambiguous, which is the point of the poem. What do we mean when we say "*Us*"? To what groups do we see ourselves belonging? How do we form a collective identity? What separates us, or joins us, one to another? This questioning links the poem to Zephaniah's "*We Refugees*", which also asks questions **about identity and belonging**.

The poem is also **a love poem**, although this is not evident until the penultimate stanza, when we realise that the speaker is addressing another person, not the reader, and he wonders if the two of them can become "*us*". Kunial shows that **belonging to someone is as important** as belonging to a community or place.

Form, structure and language

The poem is formed by seven three-line stanzas, or *tercets,* with a single line to conclude, where the questioning about belonging in the preceding stanzas is resolved into an expression of "*hope*" that the speaker can belong to one person. It is written in loose *hexametres,* with six stressed beats in each line, although the pattern of stresses varies. This, and the frequent use of *enjambment*, gives the poem a deceptively conversational tone, when in fact it is highly structured.

This is not an easy poem to understand. Ideas flow in succession, like the *metaphor* of the waves, from stanza to stanza, shifting like the concept of *"us"* and *"I"* which Kunial explores. He also uses *typography* to make subtle jokes and puns, as well as to signal the shift in **stanza five** from the general to the personal. This use of *typography* to add a layer of meaning can be compared with both Nichols's and Blakemore's poems.

Stanza one opens colloquially with *"If you ask me"*, as if addressing the reader as *"you"* and continuing a conversation. The speaker suggests that the idea of *"us"* is not fixed. Like waves (*"undulations"*) people gather and release, reaching out to others like the sea reaches between coastlines. The idea of "reaching" out is conveyed by the use of the *enjambment* between the first stanza and the next: *"reach out to/the next;"*

In **stanza two**, he explores this idea by referring to his own experience growing up in the Midlands, where he was simultaneously *"us"* – a member of the community – and *"me"* when he was singled out by his ethnicity. He was asked by his own community, although born in Britain, where he *"was from."*

In **stanza three**, he compares this experience to that of football fans who are both individuals (*"I"*) and part of a larger "*us*" called "*Liverpool*". They act together to make an actual "*Mexican wave*" which travels around the football ground, with a feeling of elation ("*cresting…the wave*") that they are together, both "*we*" and "us".

Stanza four continues the *metaphor* of the waves for unity, as it reaches from one end to the other of the stadium ("*shore-like state/two places at once*"). However, as he faces the fans at the opposite end of the pitch, the fans from the other team, he feels dispirited that they will become separate from this temporary "*us*".

In **stanza five**, the "*us*" becomes personal, as shown by the *typography*; the "us" is no longer *italicised*. He is addressing a lover and talking about their relationship, about which he is "*unsure*". The phrase "*colour me*" is a colloquial expression meaning "call me", a punning reference to his ethnicity. He feels that, somehow, he hasn't managed to quite "*stretch*" (or "reach", linking back to the wave metaphor) from "I" to "us".

Stanza six continues the idea of people as "*waves*", but his words lack the power to bring them together as one. In line 17, Kunial puns using the *typography*. By separating the word "*here*" with commas – "*I hope you get, here,*" - he gives the sentence two meanings. The first is that he hopes that the beloved will join him "*here*", and the second that the beloved understands: "*I hope you get…where I am coming from.*" He repeats the idea of "*hope*" as if he is powerless to make the two into one "us" as he stands between "*love/And loss*", the *enjambment* straddling the next stanza.

In **stanza seven**, he seems wary of showing the depth of his feeling, describing himself as "*stranded*", as if beached, a lone wave in a "*universe*" of "*I*". This wave imagery can be compared with the idea of the man in "*Island Man*" heaving himself onto the shore. Kunial then expresses his hope that from now on he will be able to say "*Us*", positioning it at the beginning of the line to show its importance.

The **final line** expresses his hope that although the idea of the two becoming "us" might be a stretch of the imagination, it will prove to be not far from the truth.

In Wales, wanting to be Italian – Imtiaz Dhakher

Context

Imtiaz Dharker was born in Lahore, Pakistan in 1954 but came to England as a baby. She is frequently anthologised for GCSE and appears regularly at *"Poetry Live"*, the annual reading of poetry by authors selected for inclusion in the GCSE syllabus. In 2014, she was awarded the Queen's Gold Medal for Poetry. Reportedly, she turned down the offer of the post of Poet Laureate, to replace Carol Ann Duffy, in 2019. As well as a poet, she is an artist, often drawing on paper in Indian ink and using text, and she illustrates all her collections. Examples can be seen on her website.

Her poetry often reflects her multi-culturalism. She describes herself as someone who *"grew up a Muslim Calvinist in a Lahori household in Glasgow and was adopted by India and married into Wales."* She now spends her time between London and Mumbai. This poem is taken from the 2014 collection *"Over the Moon"*.

Themes

Dharker explores the attraction of being someone else, of swapping your identity with that of someone from another country and a different culture. It is something she imagined in her own youth, perhaps, wondering what it would be like to adopt one of the many cultures amongst which she grew up, or to explore new ones.

Certainly, the poem recalls moments from her own teenage years, with references to where she lived growing up, and the popular culture of the 1960s and 70s, as well as where she "married into" – India and Wales.

In this poem, Dharker sees the world elsewhere as a more exciting and glamorous place than the one which she inhabits. This "elsewhere" feeds the imagination and fulfils a desire for excitement and "difference". This is in contrast to the tone of Blakemore's poem, where she expresses contentment in her home patch, or Nichols's where the Island Man wishes simply to be back where he belongs, or Zephaniah's where he imagines the pain of displaced people. The romantic appeal of these other cultures to Dharker suggests that she is more comfortable with her own identity than Chingonyi or Antrobus.

Form, structure and language

The poem is in four stanzas of *free verse*. It is written in a *colloquial* style, the language of everyday speech, similar to the style of Kunial's *"Us"*. As if she is having a conversation with the reader, Dharker asks a series of rhetorical questions, wondering whether wanting to walk in someone else's shoes is a unique or a shared fantasy.

Stanza one opens with Dharker asking if there is a *"word"* for this desire be someone else. She thinks there must be, maybe in German, and if not, one needs to be made up. She chooses *"German"* because, unlike English, German creates words by running a number of separate meanings together to create a new word – what we call a *"portmanteau"* word. She then makes up two possible new words. The first literally means: *"a desire to belong to a foreign land"* and the next *"a wish to swap around the country you belong to"*.

In **stanza two**, she again searches for a word and gives an example of what she means - living in Glasgow (where Dharker was brought up) and wanting to be French. She equates being French with being exotic, her view no doubt influenced by French films of the late 1960s-early 1970s starring Brigitte Bardot, who was famous for the way her lips formed a *"pout"*.

In **stanza three**, she asks if anyone else has felt the same as she does, giving another example. This time, she refers to Bombay, or Mumbai as it is now called, to where she eloped in her early twenties to marry Anil Dharker, a Hindu, giving birth to a daughter. "Freddie Mercury", lead singer of the 1970s band Queen, was born in Zanzibar.

In the **final stanza**, which is longer, she reverts to her original question, trying to name this wish to be someone else. This time she refers to living in Wales, to where she moved on her second marriage, to Simon Powell, in the mid-2000s. She imagines herself there at the age of sixteen, wanting to be in Italy. Again, drawing on the cinema, she wants to be able to be dramatic, applauding *"Beautiful!"*, ride an Italian moped (*"Vespa"*), smoke languorously with style and wear the kind of fashionable shoes which look fabulous, but are *"impossible"* to walk in.

Kumukanda – Kayo Chingonyi

Context

Kayombo (Kayo) Chingonyi was born in Zambia in 1987 and moved to Britain when he was six, after his father died. He has lived in Newcastle, London and Essex. The death of his mother when he was 13 is recalled in this poem. He studied at the Universities of Sheffield and Royal Holloway. In 2018, he took up a professorship at Durham University.

Chingonyi was awarded the annual Geoffrey Dearmer prize, for the best poem published in *"The Poetry Review"* written by a poet who doesn't yet have a full collection, in 2011. The poem is taken from Chingonyi's first full length collection of the same name, published in 2017 which won the Dylan Thomas prize in 2018 for the best literary work by a writer under 39, the age of Thomas when he died. *"Under Milk Wood"* by Thomas, given to Chingonyi by a teacher, influenced the young poet. In 2018, he was recipient of the Somerset Maugham Award for young writers. Chingonyi is a fellow of the Complete Works programme for Diversity and Quality in British Poetry.

Themes

In a recent essay, Chingonyi has written: *'To be both British and Zambian is to be neither one or the other. It is a hybrid way of being that means I can't be accepted by either 'side'. In the space of the poem, though, I can be both."*[27]

"*Kumukanda*" is the name given to the tribal rites of passage that young Zambian boys of the Luvale people must undergo before they become men. He learned of it from an aunt and says it: *"opened up a space in my work to write about this feeling of loss which attends moving from one place to another."*

Feelings of alienation and dislocation are shared with the Island Man in Nichols's poem, who also lives between two worlds, and by Antrobus in "*Jamaican British*". In a different context, the people in Zephaniah's "*We Refugees*" are also displaced from their homelands.

Chingonyi also explores themes of **masculinity and male tribalism**, both in his birthplace and in England, with his references to initiation rites in Zambia and his relationship with his mother's partner in England.

Form, structure and language

Chingonyi has said "*the most formalist poetry I have been exposed to is rap lyrics. They are hyper-metrical, the rhyme schemes are intricate and the levels of allusion, and allusive play, in the average rap song is staggering.*"[28] Chingonyi combines literary poetic forms with this oral tradition, including rap, grime and hip-hop influences in his poetry. Whilst this poem is apparently in *free verse,* the line lengths are fairly regular and have

---

[27] The full article from which this is taken can be found here: https://literature.britishcouncil.org/writer/kayo-chingonyi
[28] https://www.theguardian.com/books/2018/may/28/kayo-chingonyi-poet-dylan-thomas-prize

a predominantly seven-stress rhythm. *Enjambment* is used frequently place emphasis and guide the reader thematically.

The poem is in three *sestets*[29]. The first stanza considers *rites of passage* in a boy's journey to manhood amongst the Luvale people; the second, his own rite of passage in England, including the death of his mother; the third imagines an *"alternate"* Kayo, still in Zambia, meeting him and wondering what he would make of this man who writes in an alien language.

In **stanza one**, the poet reflects on the rites of passage he would have experienced had he remained in Zambia, which included a ceremonial dance around the village. Chingonyi uses *enjambment* between *"edge/of a village"* to show the "loop" of their ritual dance. He would be considered still a child (*"unfinished"*) by his father's family (*"Tata"*) as he had failed to complete the ritual of being reborn as an adult.

In **stanza two**, Chingonyi describes his own "rite of passage" in England, which was gradual, and painful, rather than ceremonial, and tied to his mother's declining ill-health and eventual death when he was 13, the age that in many religions marks the onset of adulthood . Chingonyi creates an ambiguity over the *"I chose a yellow suit"* by placing the words at the beginning of the sentence and at the end of the line, using *enjambment* to lead us to *"And white shoes"*, delaying *"I buried her in"* to create a shock that it is her

---

[29] Six-line stanzas

burial "*suit*", not his own, that he has to choose, whilst still effectively a child.

A further "*initiation*" into the adult, and masculine, world comes when, instead of the much-needed hug the child wishes from his mother's partner ("*the man I almost grew to call/ dad*"), he is given a formal handshake, as if he were an adult, both repressing their natural feelings and adopting British customs. Notice also the placing of "*dad*" at the beginning of the line, to emphasise the shift from the Luvale "*Tata*" of the first stanza to the childlike English colloquialism.

In **stanza three**, he imagines an "*alternate self*", who never left Zambia, confronting the self that left as a child. He wonders what this "*alternate self*" would make of someone who has left behind his birth language, adopted a new language, and now uses it to write in a way that is alien to to this "*alternate self*", as if he is pretending to be something he is not ("*literary pretensions*"). He asks, rhetorically, if they would be equally strange to each other and whether his "*alternate self*" would be puzzled, talking to him in the language of his ancestry, that stretches back for generations.

Chingonyi seems to be asking how long it takes, how many generations, to lose your birth right – your sense of belonging to the people and culture into which you were born.

Jamaican British – Raymond Antrobus

Context

Raymond Antrobus describes himself on Twitter as *"Poet. Teacher. Hackney lad."* He was born in 1986 in Hackney, north-east London, to an English mother and Jamaican father who emigrated to find work in the 1960s. In his early years, Antrobus struggled at school as his deafness went undiagnosed until he was six. He aspired to be a writer from an early age and started performing his poetry as part of the London Slam scene in his early twenties.

In 2018, he won the Geoffrey Dearmer prize for his poem *"Sound Machine"*, and in March 2019 the Ted Hughes Prize for his collection *"The Perseverance"*. This poem comes from his 2017 collection *"To Sweeten Bitter"*.

Aaron Samuels is an African-American Jewish poet who writes about identity. In his poem *"Broken Ghazal"*, he plays with ideas of being *"black-jewish"*:

"Kink hair & a wide nose / that's gotta be black, jewish"

Antrobus takes this poem as a spring-board (*"after Aaron Samuels"*) for his own poem exploring being *"Jamaican British"*.[30]

---

[30] The full poem can be read here: http://www.radiuslit.org/2013/02/22/three-poems-by-aaron-samuels/

Themes

Like Chingonyi, Antrobus writes about a *"hybrid way of being"*, caught between two identities. He shows how his ethnicity – *"Jamaican British"* - is fluid, changing in response to other people's expectations, in much the same way as Samuels shows how the epithets *"black, jewish"* are used as an insult, or badge of honour, depending on perspective.

This is in contrast to Dharker, who explores the attraction of being someone else, of swapping your identity with that of someone from another country and a different culture. However, she writes from the perspective of someone who seems to have come to terms with the influences of different cultures, presenting a single identity to the outside world.

Form, structure and language

The literary terminology of classic poetry cannot be readily used to describe the modern poetic forms emerging from the young BME poets, such as *dub* or *rap*. Rhythm, or beat, are important, but do not necessarily conform to traditional metrics. Many of the poems are made to be read aloud, so stress on individual words, rhymes (particularly *internal rhymes*) and line length, or syllable count, create the structure of the poems. The poem, read by Antrobus, can be heard here:
https://www.youtube.com/watch?v=M5HIJqdMM1g

The poem is written in eight *couplets*, with each line of roughly similar syllable length. A number end with *identical rhymes* – the same word repeated at the end for rhyming, rather than rhetorical, effect. [31]. Read aloud, he places subtle emphasis and pauses to point up the irony of being neither one nor the other or both, depending on perspective.

The **first couplet** opens with a declarative statement which sets out the argument of the poem. *"Some people"* point to his anglicised physical features, using these to define his ethnicity and denying his mixed race. Antrobus uses the repeated *"Jamaican British"* to create an *identical rhyme* at the end of the lines – ironically, as the point of the poem is that people's view of him is not identical, but varies depending on whether they themselves identify as black or white.

In the **second couplet**, he notes that others see him as claiming to be *"black"*, whilst his (white) fellow students ask him to *"choose"* between being *"Jamaican"* and being *"British"*, the comma showing the separation between the two and the question demanding that he *"choose"*.

The **third couplet** gives examples of what he is called from different perspectives. The first line refers to him as being of mixed race in pejorative terms. *"Half-caste"* originates from India, which still divides society by *"caste"*, a strict social/economic hierarchy. To be *"half-caste"* is to be the child of parents of different *"castes"*. A *"mule"* is the offspring of a male horse and a female

---

[31] Repetition at the end of a clause for rhetorical effect – to create emphasis for example – is called *epiphora*.

donkey. *"House slave"* is a reference to slaves in the Colonial era who were employed only in the house. The second line switches perspective to his British identity, as a light-skinned, heterosexual male which bestows on him "white privilege".

In the **fourth couplet,** he "adopts" his Jamaican heritage, speeding up the rhythm, using non-standard grammar and listing typical Jamaican foods. *"callaloo"* is a dish based on a green leafy vegetable flavoured with onion, garlic, tomatoes, thyme and Scotch bonnet pepper; *"plantains"* are like large bananas; *"jerk chicken"* is flavoured with spices such as allspice, scotch bonnet chilies, cinnamon and thyme. Eating these foods means he can declare *"I'm Jamaican"*. These dishes are alien to British cuisine; by enslaving the African-Americans, they suppressed their cuisine.

In **couplet five**, he has a fight with a boy, the positioning of the word *"Jamaican"* at the end of the line perhaps creating deliberate confusion. On the one hand, it suggests that the boy is Jamaican, who fights Antrobus because he is a "white" boy. This seems to be confirmed in the next line, as Antrobus goes home to his father and rails bitterly against *"all dem Jamaicans"*, ironically using the dialect *"dem"* instead of *"them"*, again showing confusion as he proclaims his Britishness. On the other, the "Jamaican" could be referring to himself, and the fight provoked by him being seen as "black".

The reaction of his father in **couplet six** is to use a metaphor to encourage him to embrace his whole self -

both parts of his heritage. He cannot hate something which is part of himself and makes him what he is. However, when he takes him to Jamaica, his son uses a British passport, in apparent contradiction of his Jamaican identity.

In **couplet seven**, on his arrival in Jamaica he acquires a new nickname – *"Jah-English"*. *"Jah"* is the Rastafarian name for "God", as in Hebrew "Yahwe", showing how Antrobus's Englishness sets him apart as special and makes them *"proud"*. He links this *"British"* part of him to the earlier stanzas by repeating the word at the end of each line.

In the **final couplet,** he summarises the contradictions in his ancestry. He comes from both the slaves that worked on the English plantations in the Caribbean - and the owners of those plantations ; his ancestors from the Caribbean fought for the British in the Second World War. How is he going to *"serve"* his mixed heritage when he is at war with himself?

My Mother's Kitchen – Choman Hardi

Context

Choman Hardi is the youngest daughter of Kurdish poet, Ahmed Hardi, and was born in 1974 in Iraqi Kurdistan. In 1975, the family fled to Iran in the aftermath of the Algiers Accord of 1975 which was meant to resolve border disputes between Iraq and Iran, but also to quell Kurdistan rebels seeking independence. She returned to Iraq in 1979, under an armistice, but less than ten years later her family fled again, escaping chemical warfare unleashed on the Kurds during the Anfal Campaign led by the Ba'ath Party in Iraq.[32]

In 1993, Hardi came to England with her family as a refugee, where she attended Oxford, London and Kent Universities. Initially, she wrote poems in Kurdish; her first book of poetry in English, *"Life for Us"*, from which this poem is taken, was published in 2004. This poem marks her mother's return to Iraq at the end of the Iraq war of 2003 to reclaim the house they left behind, which had been occupied by a member of the Ba'ath party, and was little more than a ruin before the family restored it. Hardi returned to Iraq in 2014 to take up a post at the American University in her home-town, Sulaymaniyah or Siemani.

Themes

---

[32]Hardi's account of this time can be found here: https://www.eadt.co.uk/ea-life/why-i-had-to-flee-my-country-1-77247

Hardi explores the refugee experience through the life of her mother, repeatedly displaced from her home. In an introduction to the poem in *The Poetry Archive*, she writes:

"This poem was written in 2003 in the aftermath of the war in Iraq and my parents decided to go home, so my mother was packing her stuff to go. And I only realised what a mess my mother's kitchen was when I met my mother-in-law, a very elegant lady from South Devon who has inherited glassware from her parents. And then I realised actually that my mother's kitchen is very much an immigrant's kitchen."

On the same website, she usefully voices the theme of "**identity**" and the refugee experience explored also by Antrobus, Nichols and Zephaniah. An extract reads:

"Writers who have come from one country and live in another, or have come from one community or one culture and live in another, can have dual identities. I guess I can be called a British poet, because I write in English, and my literature falls in line with the development of English literature. But I also can be a Kurdish poet, because much of what I write is about Kurdishness and reconstructing Kurdishness in English. I can be claimed by both, and I am very happy to do that, because I think there isn't a fixed label that any person or any writer should have really. It's a very fluid thing, identity, and I am very comfortable with being either, or both."

Form, structure and language

A recording of Hardi reading the poem can be found here: https://www.poetryarchive.org/poem/my-mothers-kitchen

The poem is written in three stanzas of *free verse*. The first stanza explores what her mother will leave behind her when she returns to Iraq; the second recalls that she has left homes behind before; the third reflects on her mother's stoic[33] response to displacement from her homes.

The opening line of **stanza one** is ambiguous; it sounds as if "*inherit*" may refer to her mother's death and the belongings that she will pass down to her daughter. The glasses are of all different shapes; her plates do not match; the cups have been bought randomly. The pots are "*rusty*" because she throws nothing away – the inference is that she may not get another. Her advice to her daughter not to buy her own things is because she knows that she is going to leave, and her daughter can have her belongings. .

In **stanza two** it is revealed that the "*inherit*" means not that she has died, but because her mother is moving back to her "*home*". The mismatched crockery and the rusty pots are because she has never really settled in her new "homes" always mindful that she may have to move on. This "*escape*" is not from a war zone but from the countries she has lived in when displaced from her own. For the "*first time*" she is not moving away from

---

[33] *Stoic* means being able to endure suffering without complaint

her home, but back to it. She is looking forward to reclaiming her birth right, even though she is elderly. Hardi pays tribute to her mother's optimism in the face of experience by placing the line *"This is her ninth time"* at the end of the stanza – she has been here before, many times.

In **stanza three**, Hardi reflects on her mother's attitude to what has happened to her. Her stoicism in the face of loss is conveyed by the repeated *"She never…"* She never complains about her loss of *"furniture"* or *"things"*, the material objects that she gathered around her as she moved from place to place. The only thing she regrets losing is a living thing – a grape vine that *"spreads"* over her *"porch"*. This is something that she cherished, tending it and watching it grow and which cannot be moved or replaced. Her daughter knows that this is something that cannot be passed on to her – it is an irreplaceable loss.

In the image of the grape vine, something which is bound to the country where it grows, Hardi is using a *metaphor* for the sorrow of being torn up by your roots and moved to an alien country. People, like trees, cannot thrive in a foreign environment, however hard they try.

The Emigrée – Carol Rumens

Context

Carol Rumens is a British poet and academic, born in South London. On her website, she says of herself: "*I would ... describe myself simply as someone who loves language, and who tries to make various things with it – poems, chiefly, but also essays, plays, translation, occasional fiction and journalistic odds and ends.*" She writes the daily blog in *The Guardian* on the Poem of the Day. Rumens has made the literature of Central and Eastern Europe a particular interest and translates from the Russian.

This *dramatic monologue* [34] was written in 1993, placing it at the time of the break-up of Yugoslavia, which resulted in the Croatian War of Independence (1991 – 1995) and the Bosnian conflict (1992 – 1995). The former, particularly, resulted in the displacement of an estimated 500,000 people. Details in the poem, however, suggest that it may refer to a city in the Middle East, particularly with the recurring image of it bathed in "*sunlight*" and being "*white*". This suggests a setting during the Gulf War of 1990-1991. Rumens leaves the identity of the Emigrée's homeland unspecified, making it applicable to all displaced people who find themselves fleeing conflict, which gives it particular relevance for today with the flight of refugees from Syria.

Themes

As in "*My Mother's Kitchen*", the main theme is **the experience of being displaced from home**, in this case a woman (*Emigrée* is the feminine form of the word) who is forced to flee her homeland as a child. The poem considers **the power of memory** to recreate the past as the woman rebuilds in her imagination the city she left as a child. It also considers **the importance of place in creating identity**. This links it to Nichols's "*Island Man*" where the man returns to his homeland in his dreams. Like the mother in Hardi's poem, the victim of displacement in this poem is life-affirming. She maintains her sense of identity, by recreating her lost past.

Form, structure and language

The poem is a *dramatic monologue*, where Rumens assumes the persona of the "*Emigrée*". A *dramatic monologue* is a poem written in the voice of someone other than the poet. They adopt a *persona*, rather than speaking as themselves. This distinguishes Rumens from other poets in the collection who are writing autobiographically – such as Hardi, Zephaniah, Kunial, Dharker or Blakemore, who write in the first person. Nichols takes a third person perspective but draws on her experience as an immigrant to enter the world of the Island Man imaginatively.

The poem is written in *free verse* in three stanzas, two of eight lines and the last having nine. The additional line seems to build the negative forces crowding in on the girl, which she finally overcomes with the affirmation of "*sunlight*", which is repeated at the end of each stanza.

The poem opens in the **first stanza** as if it were a fairy tale: "*There was once…*". Young girls are often the protagonists of fairy tales, as they are essentially "coming-of-age" stories where the girl-child faces dangers and challenges as she grows towards womanhood. The girl's memory of her childhood home is invariably positive; it is always sunny, even though she is told that it could grow cold in winter. There seems to be some significance in the naming of the month, "*November*", linking it to a particular incident, which makes the cold weather a *metaphor* for conflict back at home, of which she receives "news". However, her image of the shining city is undiminished. She likens it to a "*paperweight*". A paperweight is used to hold down papers. It is made of heavy glass and often contains intricate patterns made of blown glass or even real objects such as shells and flowers. She uses the image to suggest that the memory of her city grounds her, gives her a sense of identity, and that she holds within herself a clear image of it still. In spite of the conflict raging there, for her it is still filled with "*sunlight*", so bright that it marks ("*brands*") her forever.

In the **second stanza**, she finds that as the city grows more distant in time, her memories of it grow clearer. Even while she can imagine tanks rolling through the streets and the possibilities of returning become more remote, she is recreating the lost city. She uses the image of waters closing above her to show how she is becoming physically separated from it, if not imaginatively: *"rolls/rise/waves"*. However, even though she has been separated from her homeland, her native language is growing still within her. She brought with her a few words in her native tongue, but she is continuing to develop it, building a grammatical structure. The image of the *"hollow doll"* again suggests that the poet is drawing on the culture of Russia and Eastern Europe, in recalling the "Matryoshka" nesting dolls. *"coloured molecule"* is a reference to light, which is made up of a spectrum of colours. When she has put together all the words, she will have created a language. Even though back at "home" it is now forbidden to speak it, she cannot rid herself of it, likening it to a taste on her tongue, a punning reference to language being your *"mother tongue"*. Even this taste is like *"sunlight"*.

The **third stanza** expands the idea of being unable to return to her home. She is stateless, without a passport and so cannot go back. Instead, her city comes to her in memory and imagination, as if on its own *"plane"*. This image then morphs, first into the idea of it being a *"paper"* plane that lies before her, and then into a beloved doll, that she plays with. This "companion" then shows her itself – the *"shining"* city of her imagination which takes her *"dancing"*. She then seems to contrast **her** "city" – the sunlight bright place in her imagination – with the *"city of walls"*, which has been created by the conflict. The *personification* of this *"city of walls"* becomes increasingly menacing, the walls making a "*circle*" around her, enclosing her; accusing her of betrayal as she has left it behind; accusing her of "*being dark*" where it is "*free*" – even though she knows that it is still a conflict zone. **Her** city of the imagination "*hides behind her*", as if seeking protection from a negative reality. "*They*" – the "*walls*" of the real city left behind and, by extension, the "*tyrants*" (from stanza 1, line 7) who now occupy it and have banned her language – threaten her with death, but she remains bathed in the sunlight of her remembered and imagined city, casting a shadow in front of her, attesting to its reality.

Rumen's poem requires the reader to grasp a central *conceit*[35] of the "*shining city* and follow how it is used imaginatively to explore the poet's theme. This can be challenging and ultimately, the effectiveness of the poem depends on whether the struggle to grasp the meaning is worth the effort and adds to the overall experience of reading the poem.

---

[35] A *conceit* is an elaborate metaphor

Links, Connections, Comparisons & the Unseen Poem

The exam question (the "task")

The exam question will give you a *"theme"* to discuss as a guide to which aspects of the poem(s) they want you to focus on. They will probably use the word *"Compare"*. Where possible, links and connections should be made to each poem throughout the essay, alternating between the two, for the highest marks. The examiners are less keen on one analysis followed by another, unless there is clear cross-referencing and/or there is a clearly comparative paragraph at the beginning and at the end.

What is happening in the poem?

The first task is to understand *"What is happening in the poem?"* Unless you understand this, your analysis will be meaningless. Make sure you understand what the story, incident, event or imaginative idea is that has prompted the poet to write the poem. No poem exists in a vacuum – there is always a reason for writing it. Find that reason – the inspiration which leads to the poem.

The first "link or connection" to be made is to summarise, briefly, the "story" of each poem ***and how this relates to the theme of the question***. This is the first response to *"How"* the poet has approached his subject. It is the framework around which he hangs his ideas. It is suggested that you do this in your first paragraph. It also reassures the Examiner that your analysis is not starting from an erroneous base. **Make** the "story" the first point of comparison between the texts.

What is the relevant context within which the whole poem is written?

Make any immediate comparisons of "**context**". Are the poems addressing the same themes but within **a different time-frame** (past/present, for example)? Is there any relevance of the theme to our **experience today which is different to theirs**? Are the poets writing in a particular **literary tradition**? What do you know about **the poets' lives** that is relevant and may be a cause for writing the poems? Are there any **specific events** that the poems are referring to?

Ensure that you always relate context back to the question. They do not want, for example, a history of Romantic poetry – but they do want you to show that you understand their **predominant concerns and styles** and **how this is reflected** in the poetry.

As you discuss **form, structure and language**, refer to any relevant **contextual factors that affect the choice of these elements**. For example, the use of classical or religious imagery reflecting a literary tradition or societal norms; use of language forms, such as *dialect*, that are used to convey the message of the poem.

Form, Structure and Language

A poem may have many ideas in it. Your task is to explain **how the poet has used form, structure and language to explore the theme which is the focus of the question**. Below are some of the features of the poems that you can choose to explore, both when making links, connections and comparisons between the prescribed poem and one other from the *Anthology*, AND when linking the two Unseen poems.

Remember that the highest marks are given when the analysis of form, structure and language is related to meaning and to the theme under discussion. Fewer marks are given for merely identifying techniques in isolation from meaning. The commentaries on the poems show you how to do this.

It is important that you use "*examples*" (quotes) to illustrate your argument. Never make a comment about how the poet has approached his subject without an example to illustrate. You should also ***never use a quote without then going on to talk about the quote*** itself, analysing any structural or language features in depth and ***relating this to the writer's intention***. This ensures that you are covering the assessment objective AO2 – "*showing a critical understanding of the writer's craft.*" However, comments like "*paint a picture in your mind*" or "*make the reader feel sorry for…*" are too general to gain credit at the higher levels. You need to be specific about why a writer has chosen a language or structural feature.

Theme	The question will focus on a theme. Some key themes have been identified in the commentary on the texts. Choose poems which can be linked thematically as a first choice for linking, connecting and comparing. Trying to link poems "because you know them" is not a good plan.
Context	Is there a historical /biographical /literary /political/ social-economic background that is relevant to the text and the way it is written? **How does the context of the text relate to the meaning of the text and help us to understand it?**
Narrative Voice	Who is speaking in the poem? Is it the poet, or is he speaking through someone else? Is there more than one *voice*? The narrative voice is the person who is speaking in the poem. It may be the poet (many of the poems are autobiographical) or a *persona* – an imagined speaker, as in a *dramatic monologue*. Or it may be the poet simply talking to us about an idea that he/she wishes to explore. **What does the choice of narrative voice tell us about the poet's approach to his theme or about the theme itself?**

Form	Is the poem written in a named poetic form, such as *sonnet, ode, elegy, ballad*? **What does the choice of form tell you about the subject matter or the attitude of the poet?**
Structure	How many lines are there in a stanza? How is the story arranged around these lines? What is the subject matter of each stanza? In what order has the story or happening been told to us? Are there shifts in time or place? Is there a regular rhythm? If so, what is this rhythm? Is there a regular rhyme scheme? Are *full rhymes*, *half-rhymes* and *eye-rhymes* used? Are the lines *end-stopped* – does the meaning follow the rhyme and complete at the end of each rhymed line? Does the poet use *enjambment* and *caesura* to vary the pace of the line and create a looser structure within a rigid one? What does this say about the subject matter or the poet's attitude to his subject? Is it in free verse, with no discernible regular rhyme or rhythm? How has the poet chosen where to end the lines? **How does the choice and use of structure relate to meaning and what is the effect on the reader?**

Language	Is the language formal or informal? Does it sound conversational, confiding, reminiscent, musing, purposeful…? What is the tone? Sorrowful, regretful, angry, puzzled, triumphant…? What is the proportion of *vernacular* (words of common speech) to Latinate (polysyllabic, Latin derivations, "difficult")? Is the language descriptive, factual, plain, colloquial …? Is the language literal, or does it have many *similes* and *metaphors*, or *personification*? What kinds of *imagery* are used: religious, naturalistic, mechanistic…? Are there particular words used which are unusual? Archaic, *dialect*, slang…? **How does the choice and use of language relate to meaning and what is the effect on the reader?**

A Note on Metre

Rhythm in English Verse

Rhythm in English verse is dependent on the **pattern** and **number** of *stressed* and *unstressed* syllables in a line. This is called ***metre***. The name given to the ***metric line*** depends on **a)** the pattern of *stressed* and *unstressed* beats in the ***metric feet*** and b) the number of ***metric feet*** in a line. If the pattern changes in a line, the predominant pattern is used to define it.

Pattern

Each pattern of *stressed* and *unstressed* syllables has its own name. In the examples, the *stressed* syllables (or *beats*, as in music) are highlighted. The symbol "/" divides the line into its *metric feet*.

*"The **mor**/ning **road**/ is **thronged**/ with **mer**/ry **boys**"*

Here, there are five *metric feet* in each line, each with the pattern "light/**HEAVY**" or "ti-**TUM**". This makes it a *metric line* of five *iambs* – *iambic pentametre*.

Iamb – unstressed, stressed (ti-**TUM**). *"It **is**/ the **first**/ mild **day**/ of **March**"* which is a regular *iambic* line. It is the most common *foot* found in English poetry. Wordsworth's line above is *iambic tetrametre* – four feet of *iambs*.

Trochee – stressed, unstressed (**TUM**-ti). *"**Mild** the/ **mist** up/**on** the/ **hill**"* which is *trochee, trochee, trochee,* and an unfinished *trochee* – or *catalectic* ending.

Spondee – stressed, stressed (**TUM-TUM**). "**Love, now/** a **un/**i**ver/**sal **truth**" which is *spondee, iamb, iamb, iamb*

Dactyl – stressed, unstressed, unstressed (**TUM**-ti-ti). "**Half** a league, **half** a league" which is *dactyl, dactyl.* Another example of a *dactyl* is in the word *"**Li**verpool"*

Anapest – unstressed, unstressed, stressed (ti-ti-**TUM**) "The As**syr**ian des**cend**ed like the **wolf** on the **fold**", which is a regular *anapaestic* rhyme.

Amphibrach – unstressed, stressed, unstressed (ti-**TUM**-ti) as in "*to**ma**to/po**ta**to".* This is rarely found, but Landon uses it frequently in the middle of the line:

"From **whence/** we **took/** our **fu**ture// to **fa/**shion **as** /we **might**"

Counting *metric feet*

In Wordsworth's lines above, there are four *metric feet.* The number of *metric feet* is given a name derived from Greek metrics, as below:

The numbers of *feet* in a line are called:

Trimetre – 3	Hexametre - 6
Tetrametre - 4	Heptametre - 7
Pentametre – 5	Octametre – 8

A *catalectic* line is one where the last, or first, part of a metric foot is missing. This is most clearly seen in Bridges' poem which is in *trochaic trimetre catalectic* :

Calm and/ *gent*le/ *stream*!
Known and/ *loved* so/ *long*,

Metric Forms or Names (given in order of prevalence)

Iambic pentametre – is the commonest metric form in English and comprises a *metric line* of *five iambic feet*. Variation is given by the use of other *feet*, which can give the verse the sound of natural speech rhythms. However, the *five foot, iambic pattern* is always underlying.

NOTE: you will hear people describe *iambic pentametre* as containing ten unstressed/stressed *syllables*. This is not the case. **It has nothing to do with the number of syllables** – only the number and type of the *feet*.

Bl*ank verse* is *unrhymed iambic pentametre,* commonly used by Shakespeare, but also by Seamus Heaney and other modern poets who write in a classic tradition. It is NOT the same as *free verse*, which has no regular rhythm or rhyme.

Iambic tetrametre is four *iambic* beats in a line, as used by Wordsworth in *"To My Sister"*:

"There **is**/ a **bles**/sing **in**/ the **air**,"

Tetrametre is also the rhythm of many nursery rhymes. We describe this as "sing-song" as it is common in songs and light verse. The four-beat **iambic tetrametre** line may alternate with a three-beat **iambic trimetre** as in **common** or **ballad metre,** used by Bronte in *"Mild the mist"*.

This *metre* can be used **ironically** by poets when dealing with a serious subject, so watch out for a deliberate mismatch between the sing-song rhythm of *ballad metre* and the subject matter to make an ironic point.

End-stopping is where the sense of the line, contained in a clause or sentence, ends at the end of the line, where the *metric line* ends, as in Clare's *"Sunday Dip"*:

"The boldest ventures first and dashes in,"

This tends to emphasise the rhyme, making it more insistent.

Enjambment is the opposite of *end-stopped*. The sense of the line continues onto the next line, often landing on a stressed beat, to emphasise the first word of the line, and enhance meaning, as here in Clare's *"Sunday Dip"*, where the run-on line leads us from *"wade"* to *"dance"*. It propels the verse forwards, making it flow, even if there is a regular rhyme scheme:

*"They run to seek the shallow pit, and wade
And dance about the water in the shade."*

Free verse is a modern form of poetry that has no regular *rhythm* or *rhyme*. This is not to say that makes no use of either. If there were neither rhythm nor rhyme throughout, then one might as well call it prose, divided up into arbitrary lines. *Free verse* frequently uses *enjambment* and *caesura* to guide the reader through the argument and create rhythmic and rhyming effects.

Printed in Great Britain
by Amazon